D1119884

Market maze
33305233831761
0jn   12/02/15

Market Maze

ROXIE MUNRO

Holiday House / New York

To Ann Munro Wood, Rue Judd, Gunilla Gustafsson,
Birgitta Carlo, and all my other friends
who love to garden

Copyright © 2015 by Roxie Munro
All Rights Reserved
HOLIDAY HOUSE is registered in the U.S. Patent and Trademark Office.
Printed and Bound in October 2014 at Toppan Leefung, DongGuan City, China.
The artwork was created with India ink and colored acrylic inks on paper.
www.holidayhouse.com
First Edition
1 3 5 7 9 10 8 6 4 2

Library of Congress Cataloging-in-Publication Data
Munro, Roxie.
Market maze / Roxie Munro. — First edition.
pages cm
ISBN 978-0-8234-3092-5 (hardcover)
1. Maze puzzles—Juvenile literature.
2. Markets—Juvenile literature. I. Title.
GV1507.M3M85 2015
793.73—dc23
2013038988

How to Have Fun with This Book

All over the world, people know that the locally grown products in their farmers' markets, sometimes called greenmarkets, are the best and the freshest. In this book you can learn about different foods and the habitats and environments they come from.

Starting at the sea, follow the directions on each page. Each maze connects to the one on the next page to make one huge maze. Using roads, trails, and walkways, take the shortest route to bring the great products to the city's open-air farmers' market. Along the way, there are fun things to find and count. The answers, along with more information, can be found at the back of the book.

Visit your local farmers' market and think about where the food you eat comes from and how it gets to you.

"Good catch today!"

Guide the boat to the dock's loading area. Transfer the catch to the FISH truck, go to the fish-packing plant, and drive toward town.

FIND: **1** lighthouse, **3** wind turbines, **1** boat-loading ramp, **3** picnic tables, **1** gas pump, **2** sailboats, **1** jetty, **2** navigation buoys, **2** canoes

"It's apple-picking time!"

Drive the APPLE truck to the east orchard and collect the apples. Stop by the cider house. Next, get apples from the north and west orchards. Then head to town.

FIND: **5** deer, **1** fisherman, **1** squirrel, **1** picnic area, **13** ladders, **1** waterfall, **1** red-tailed hawk, **1** rowboat, **1** FISH truck

8

"Milk for cereal, and ice cream too"

Load the DAIRY truck at the goat-and-sheep farm. Pick up cheese at the next farm's dairy barn and hit the road to the Greenmarket!

FIND: 2 dogs, 1 raccoon, 1 bull, 1 clothesline, 2 black sheep, 1 tree house, 3 deer, 1 APPLE truck, 1 FISH truck

"Love corn on the cob!"

Pick up CORN from the barn, drive over to the corn maze, and walk through it. Drop off some corn at the roadside stand and then get on the highway.

FIND: 2 picnic areas, **2** tractors, **1** school bus, **2** bicycles, **1** corn combine, **1** DAIRY truck, **1** APPLE truck, **1** FISH truck

"Pansies are my favorite."
Take the FLOWER truck to pick up petunias,
chrysanthemums, hollyhocks, sunflowers,
hothouse roses, and then marigolds. Next,
collect cacti, orchids, hydrangeas, and
pansies. Head for town.
FIND: **3** picnic tables, **1** fountain,
2 pickup trucks, **1** CORN truck,
1 DAIRY truck, **1** APPLE truck,
1 FISH truck

"I want mine scrambled."
Load the EGG truck. Then drive to the other chicken farm's barn to pick up more eggs. Take the road to the Greenmarket.

FIND: 6 chicken coops, 1 fox, 1 swing set, 4 roosters, 1 FLOWER truck, 1 CORN truck, 1 DAIRY truck, 1 APPLE truck, 1 FISH truck

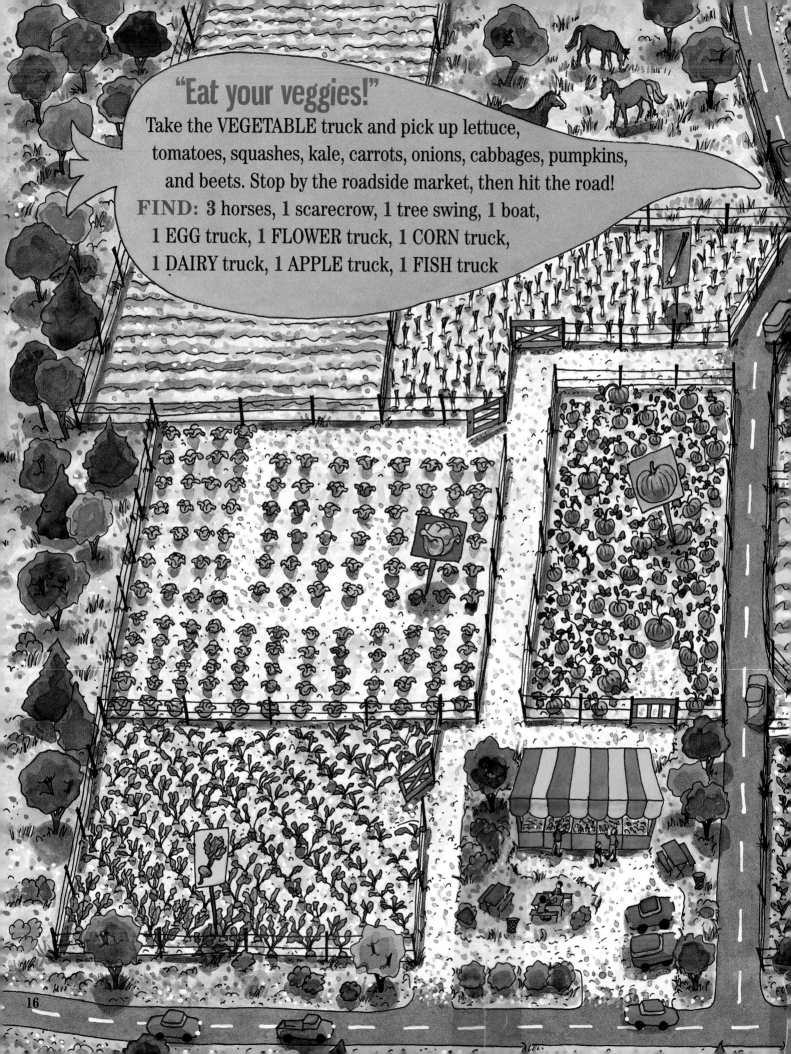

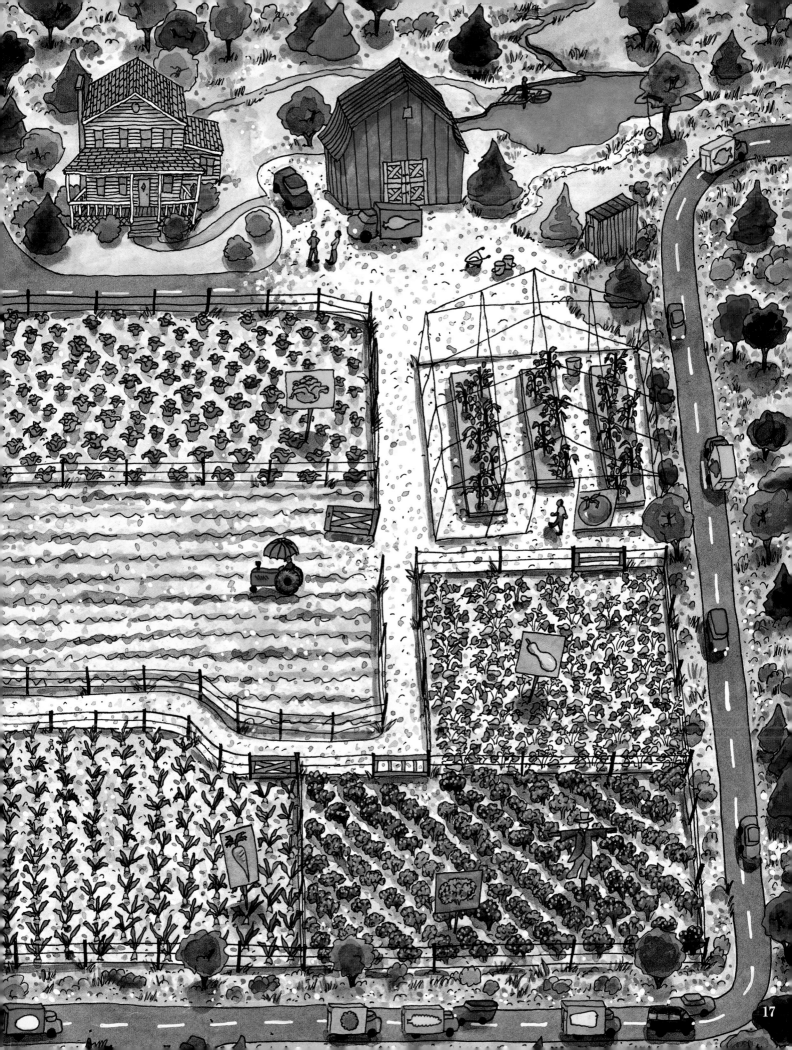

"Now for the yummies . . ."

With the BAKERY truck, pick up bread, cookies, pies, croissants, cakes, cupcakes, and doughnuts. Drive into town.

FIND: 1 train, 1 gas station, 3 picnic tables, 1 clock, 1 VEGETABLE truck, 1 EGG truck, 1 FLOWER truck, 1 CORN truck, 1 DAIRY truck, 1 APPLE truck, 1 FISH truck

"We're off on a field trip!"

The class boards the SCHOOL BUS. Go through town to visit the Greenmarket.

FIND: 1 fire station, 2 slides, 3 dogs, 1 baseball field, 1 BAKERY truck, 1 VEGETABLE truck, 1 EGG truck, 1 FLOWER truck, 1 CORN truck, 1 DAIRY truck, 1 APPLE truck, 1 FISH truck

"Let's go!"

Arrive at the PARKING LOT. Unload all the trucks and the bus, and walk to the Greenmarket entrance.

FIND: **2** window washers, **3** dogs, **2** bicycles, **1** unicycle, **1** skateboard, **1** double stroller, **1** SCHOOL BUS, **1** BAKERY truck, **1** VEGETABLE truck, **1** EGG truck, **1** FLOWER truck, **1** CORN truck, **1** DAIRY truck, **1** APPLE truck, **1** FISH truck

"Welcome!"

At the GREENMARKET, get your reusable bag at the Information Booth. Buy a dozen fresh eggs, grab a doughnut and a napkin, some colorful flowers, and get the chef's cookbook signed. Next, buy fresh fish and recycle the napkin. Get delicious apples, some goat cheese, and lots of healthy veggies. Buy a dozen ears of yellow corn. Finish your Greenmarket visit by listening to local musicians.

How does food get to your plate?

Our food comes from a variety of sources, from land and sea. Sometimes it is grown in the earth and sometimes it comes from animals. Often food is served fresh, just as it grew, but can also be cooked, baked, or combined from several products.

Food comes from different environments. We find fish in the sea or in rivers. Apples usually grow in hilly, slightly cool areas. Animals that produce milk, used also for butter and cheese, like grass and require a lot of space. Corn needs sun and grows in long rows in open fields. Flowers take special care; most can grow outside, but some, such as orchids and roses, need greenhouses to regulate conditions. We prefer "free-range" eggs and poultry, which means that chickens have space to scratch around in. Vegetables require sun and water; it's best to pick them when they are ripe and ready. Bakeries are often near towns so their products can be delivered fast and fresh. These days, schools are paying more attention to nutrition, and children are eager to learn about the food they eat. Many schools arrange day trips to farmers' markets, where, like the rest of the community, students can talk to the producers and enjoy fresh, locally grown food.

Answer Key

Pick up market goods on the **blue** path.
Get the trucks to town on the **red** path.
Things hidden on each spread are inside the **orange** rings.

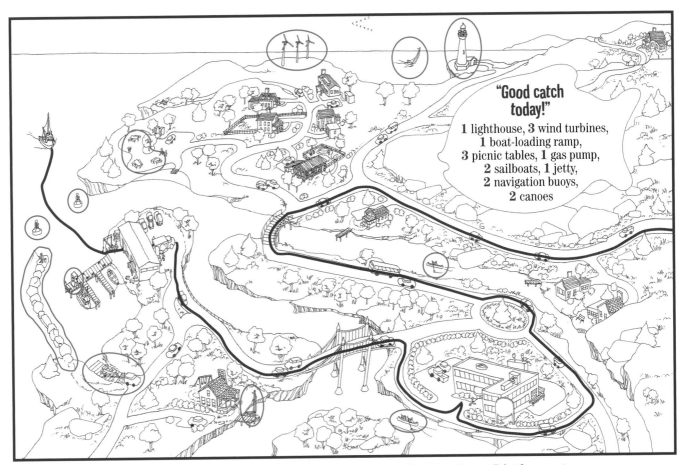

"Good catch today!"
1 lighthouse, 3 wind turbines,
1 boat-loading ramp,
3 picnic tables, 1 gas pump,
2 sailboats, 1 jetty,
2 navigation buoys,
2 canoes

Most professional fishermen get up very early and bring their catch back by dawn. It's the most dangerous job in America, but many fishermen come from generations of families doing the same work. Besides fresh fish you may find other seafood, such as shrimp, clams, lobsters, crabs, oysters, and scallops at the market.

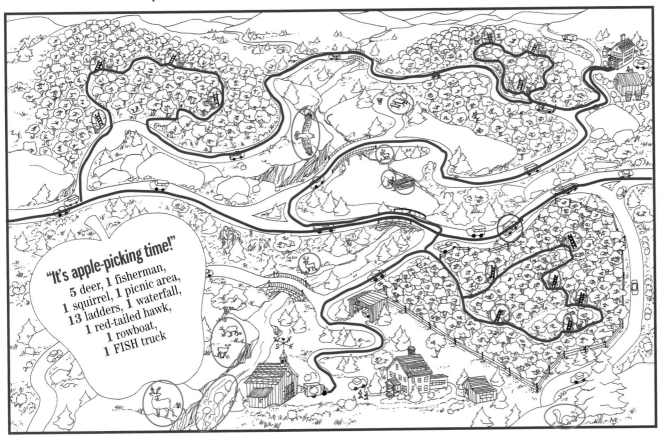

"It's apple-picking time!"
5 deer, 1 fisherman,
1 squirrel, 1 picnic area,
13 ladders, 1 waterfall,
1 red-tailed hawk,
1 rowboat,
1 FISH truck

There are hundreds of kinds of apples. Many have fun names, such as Mollie's Delicious, Golden Spy, Granny Smith, and Pink Lady. In the United States, Washington State grows the most apples, but China produces the most apples in the world. Not all apples are red; some are yellow or green. But all are good for you!

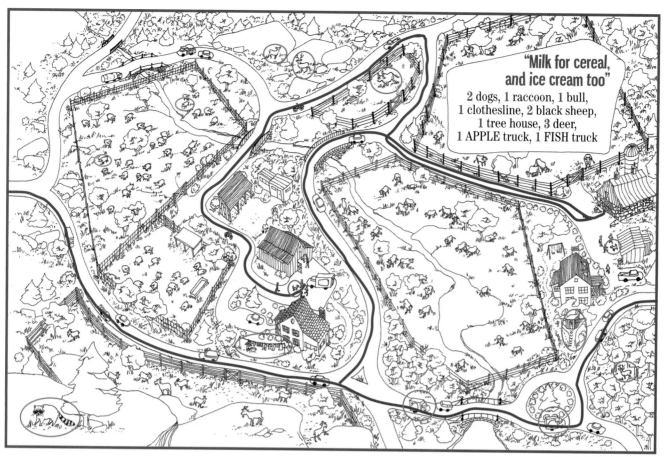

"Milk for cereal,
and ice cream too"
2 dogs, 1 raccoon, 1 bull,
1 clothesline, 2 black sheep,
1 tree house, 3 deer,
1 APPLE truck, 1 FISH truck

Dairies in the United States can have sheep or goats in addition to cows. Besides providing milk and cream they often make cheese, butter, yogurt, and even ice cream. Did you know that in some countries horse's or camel's milk is used for food? Dairy products have a lot of calcium, which is very good for your teeth and bones.

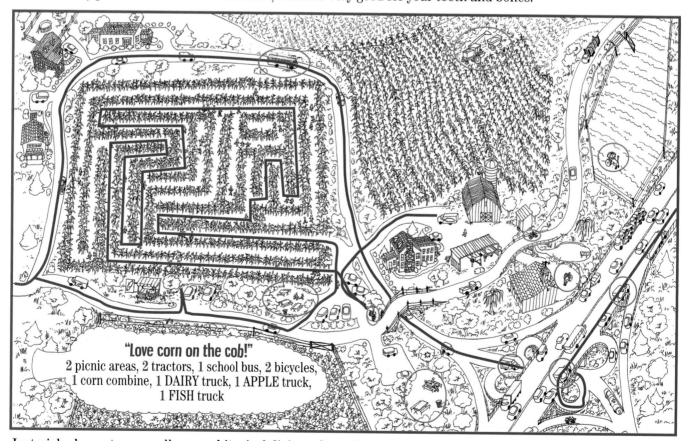

"Love corn on the cob!"
2 picnic areas, 2 tractors, 1 school bus, 2 bicycles,
1 corn combine, 1 DAIRY truck, 1 APPLE truck,
1 FISH truck

Just-picked sweet corn, yellow or white, is delicious. Some farmers, in addition to growing corn, create corn mazes for families to enjoy visiting in the late summer and fall. Most mazes are 4 to 20 acres in size. They can be complex; for example, a maze might be in the shape of a state, with paths inside. To make them, a farmer sometimes uses a GPS (Global Positioning System) on his or her tractor.

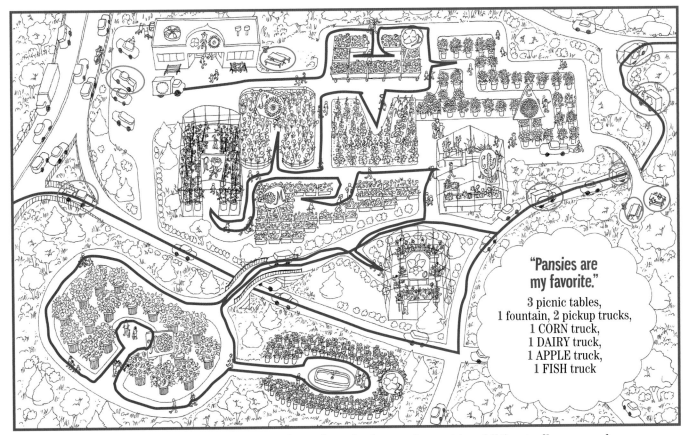

Nurseries often sell bushes, shrubs, trees, seeds, and gardening equipment in addition to flowers and vegetables. We eat or drink foods made from flowers such as roses, sunflowers, and cacti. Some flowers are annuals—you have to plant new seeds every spring. But many are perennials—you don't have to replant; they keep blooming every spring for years.

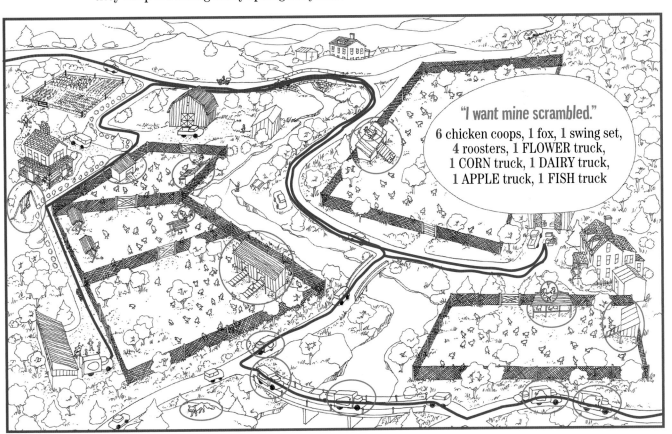

Eggs have been called "nature's perfect food." All the nutritional value is found in the yolk (the yellow center). We like them scrambled, fried, deviled, poached, and boiled, and even color them for Easter. There's no difference in taste or quality between a hen's egg that is white or brown. Besides chicken eggs, people eat duck, quail, goose, and even fish eggs (called roe or caviar).

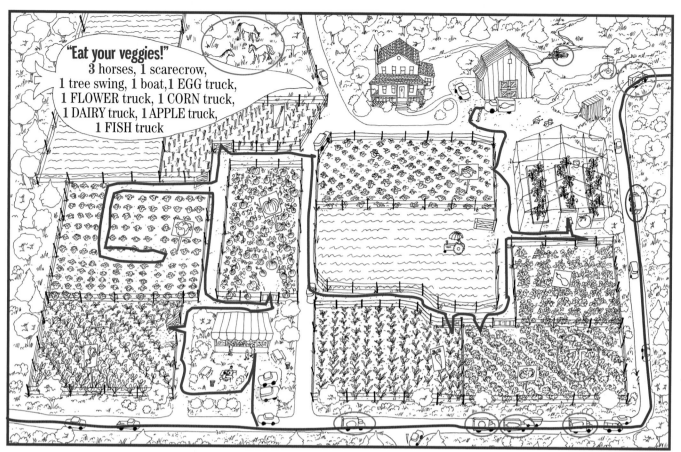

Your local farmers' market is a great place to buy fresh vegetables while they are in season. Vegetables have lots of the vitamins and minerals that your body needs to stay healthy. Carrots and pumpkins, for example, are especially good for your eyes. Spinach is also good for your eyes and helps build strong bones.

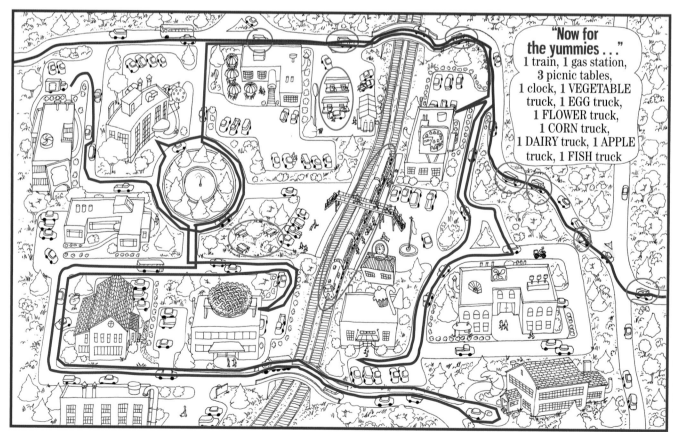

Bakers are like fishermen—many get up very early each day to go to work and make our breads and desserts. The smell of freshly baked bread or cookies is wonderful. Bakeries are kept particularly busy during holidays such as Christmas, Passover, Easter, Halloween, and Thanksgiving. Many are busy all the time for weddings and birthdays!

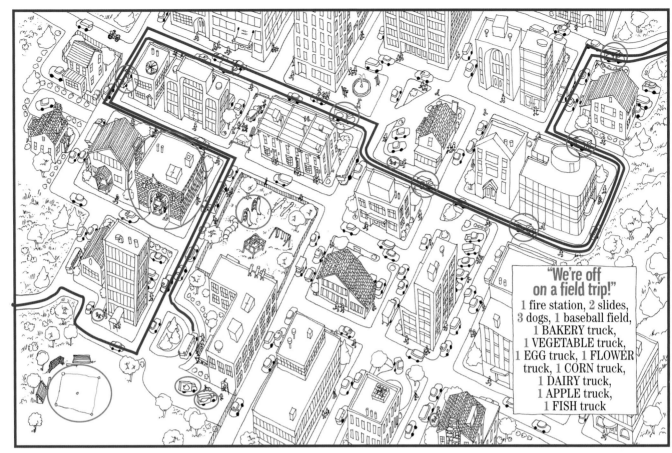

"We're off on a field trip!"
1 fire station, 2 slides,
3 dogs, 1 baseball field,
1 BAKERY truck,
1 VEGETABLE truck,
1 EGG truck, 1 FLOWER
truck, 1 CORN truck,
1 DAIRY truck,
1 APPLE truck,
1 FISH truck

Farmers' markets are great places for school classes to visit—children can talk to the producers in their booths. Students can learn about many kinds of jobs, where food comes from, the different varieties of food, and what's good for you and why. They might even get to sample some delicious products!

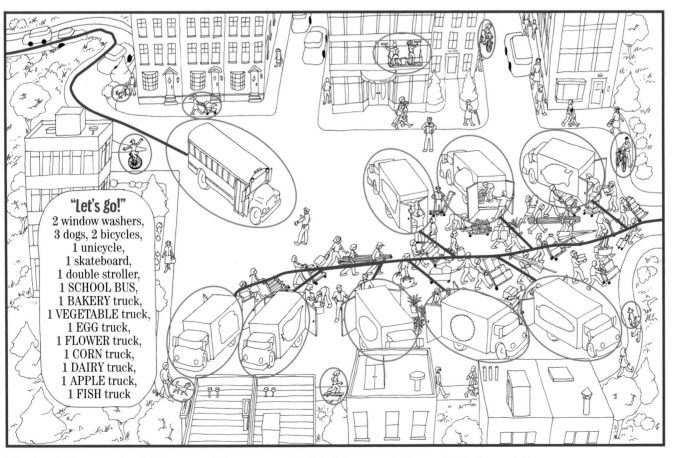

"Let's go!"
2 window washers,
3 dogs, 2 bicycles,
1 unicycle,
1 skateboard,
1 double stroller,
1 SCHOOL BUS,
1 BAKERY truck,
1 VEGETABLE truck,
1 EGG truck,
1 FLOWER truck,
1 CORN truck,
1 DAIRY truck,
1 APPLE truck,
1 FISH truck

The trucks have arrived. Everyone is busy—wonderful things are being unloaded carefully.
Soon all the farmers, bakers, fishermen, and flower growers will set up the market for the day.
And now the school bus full of curious kids arrives!

Farmers' markets (sometimes called open-air or greenmarkets) are great for a community. Producers like to sell their homemade and fresh local products directly to their customers. Visitors are happy to shop for such healthy food, taste samples, socialize, and maybe listen to live music or watch a cooking demonstration.

Find Farmers' Markets Near You

You can look up farmers' markets near you on a search page on the website of the United States Department of Agriculture (USDA). http://search.ams.usda.gov/farmersmarkets/
You can locate farmers' markets in Canada on the Farmer's Markets Canada website. www.farmersmarketscanada.ca/index.cfm

Discover When Fresh Produce Is in Season in Your Region

USDA website. http://snap.nal.usda.gov/nutrition-through-the-seasons
Field to Plate's listing of regional charts. www.fieldtoplate.com/guide.php

Learn More about Farmers and Food Suppliers

The USDA has a video and other resources about the benefits of shopping at farmers' markets.

www.nutrition.gov/farmers-markets
Interviews with farmers and suppliers at New York area farmers' markets can be found on the GrowNYC website.
www.grownyc.org/greenmarket/farmers
Climate Kids NASA's Eyes on the Earth interviews a manager of a farmers' market.
http://climatekids.nasa.gov/career-farmers-market/

Resources for Educators

The USDA's National Agricultural Library includes a list of resources for educators.

www.nal.usda.gov/educational-resources-children-parents-and-teachers
The University of Illinois Extension website also includes resources.
http://urbanext.illinois.edu/food/